DISCOVERING THE UNITED KINGDOM

ALL ABOUT
ENGLAND

BY SUSAN HARRISON

BookLife
PUBLISHING

©2020
BookLife Publishing Ltd.
King's Lynn
Norfolk PE30 4LS

ISBN: 978-1-83927-112-0

All rights reserved
Printed in Malaysia

A catalogue record for this book is available from the British Library.

Written by:
Susan Harrison

Edited by:
Grace Jones

Designed by:
Drue Rintoul

All facts, statistics, web addresses and URLs in this book were verified as valid and accurate at time of writing. No responsibility for any changes to external websites or references can be accepted by either the author or publisher.

CONTENTS

Page 4 — **WELCOME TO ENGLAND**
Page 6 — **THE HISTORY OF ENGLAND**
Page 8 — **LANDMARKS**
Page 10 — **WEATHER & LANDSCAPE**
Page 12 — **TOWNS & CITIES**
Page 14 — **THE COUNTRYSIDE & WILDLIFE**
Page 16 — **THE COASTLINE**
Page 18 — **PEOPLE**
Page 20 — **CULTURE, LEISURE & TOURISM**
Page 22 — **SPORT**
Page 24 — **TRADITIONS**
Page 26 — **QUICK QUIZ**
Page 28 — **USEFUL LINKS & PLACES TO VISIT**
Page 30 — **GLOSSARY & INDEX**

Words that look like **this** can be found in the glossary on page 30.

WELCOME TO ENGLAND

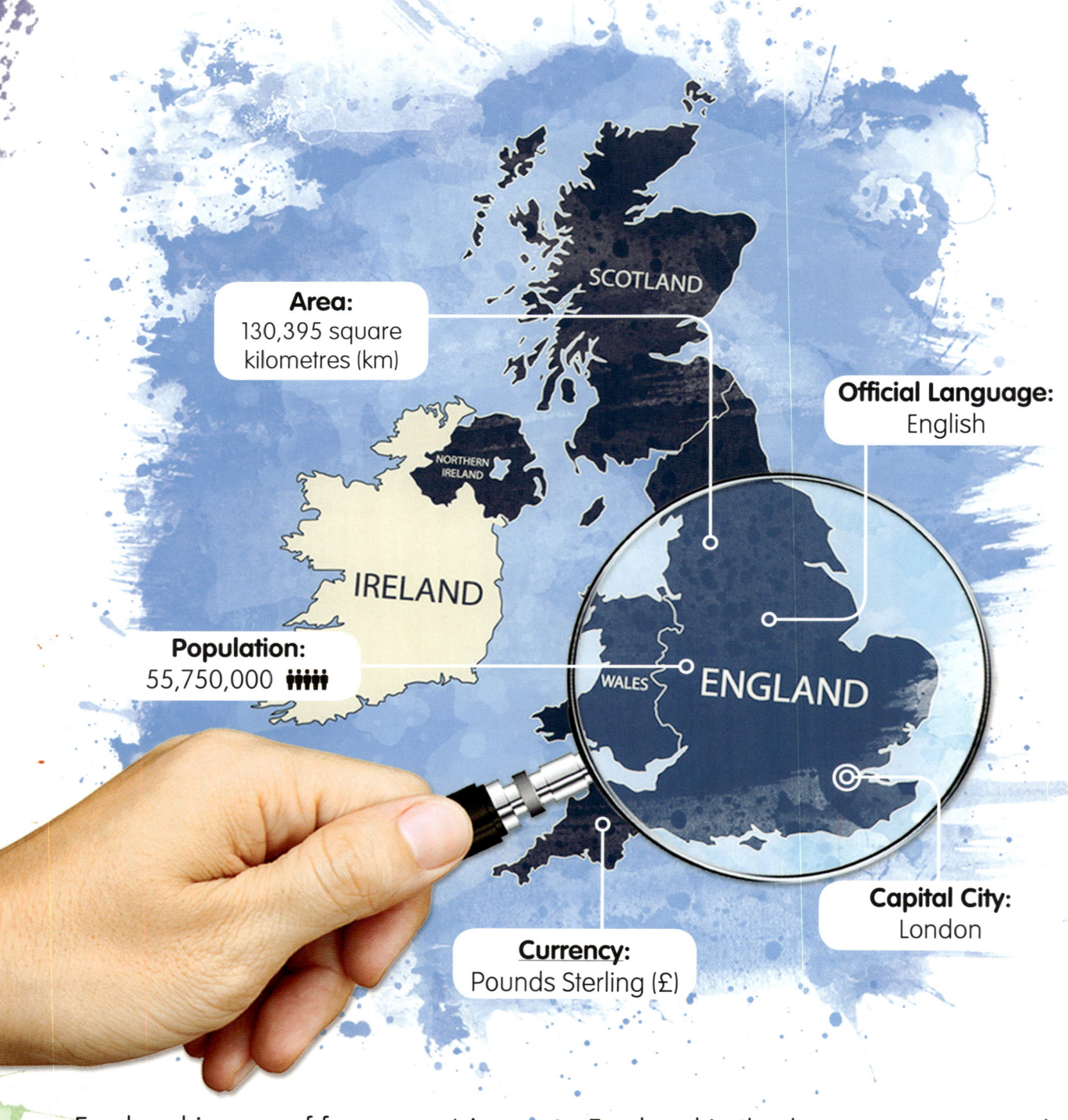

Area: 130,395 square kilometres (km)

Official Language: English

Population: 55,750,000

Currency: Pounds Sterling (£)

Capital City: London

England is one of four countries which, together with **Scotland**, **Wales** and **Northern Ireland**, form the **United Kingdom**.

England is the largest country in the UK, and is bordered by Scotland in the north, and Wales in the west. Northern Ireland is separated from England by the sea.

TAKE A LOOK www.visitbritain.com is a great website to look at to find out more about England.

ENGLAND IS A COUNTRY OF DIVERSE LANDSCAPES AND HISTORY

England has a diverse landscape, varying from rolling hills and mountains to long stretches of coastline. There are many different towns, cities and villages, too.

England is a popular place for visitors from other countries to come because of the beautiful and diverse countryside, historical sites and traditions. They also come to experience England's **culture** in the form of music, theatre, literature, art and sport.

Queen Elizabeth II is the official **Head of State** for England, and appears on many postage stamps used in the UK every day. But did you know that there is a very old law that says that it is illegal to place a postage stamp of the Queen upside down on a letter?

BIG BEN & THE PALACE OF WESTMINSTER

THE HISTORY OF ENGLAND

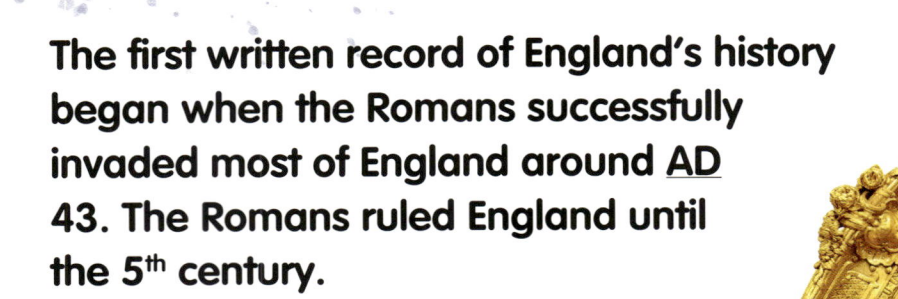

The first written record of England's history began when the Romans successfully invaded most of England around <u>AD</u> 43. The Romans ruled England until the 5th century.

Since then the country has been ruled by many different peoples, ranging from the Anglo-Saxons and Vikings, right through to Queen Elizabeth II, who is the country's longest-serving **monarch**.

ELIZABETH II IS THE LONGEST-SERVING BRITISH MONARCH.

PUBLIC BATHS, LIKE THIS ONE FOUND IN BATH, ARE A REMINDER OF THE ROMAN OCCUPATION OF BRITAIN.

43–410
Roman Britain

410–1066
Anglo-Saxons

1066–1154
Norman Britain

1154–1485
The Middle Ages

1485–1603
Tudor England

TAKE A LOOK Head to www.britishmuseum.org and www.nationaltrust.org.uk to find lots of information about the history of England.

Many bloody battles have been fought in defence of England over hundreds of years. One of the most famous battles in England's history took place in 1066. This was when William the Conqueror from Normandy fought King Harold for the crown of England and won.

Here's a little rhyme to help you remember all the kings and queens of England!

Willie, Willie, Harry, Steve,
Harry, Dick, John, Harry three;
One, two, three Neds, Richard two,
Harry's four, five, six... then who?
Edward four, five, Rich the Bad,
Two more Henry's and Ned the Lad,
Mary, Bessie, James the Vain,
Charlie, Charlie, James again...
William and Mary, Anna Gloria,
Four Georges, William and Victoria,
Edward seven next, and then,
George the fifth in 1910,
Ned the eighth soon abdicated,
Then George the sixth was coronated;
And, if you've not yet lost your breath,
Give a cheer for Elizabeth!

THE OLDEST HUMAN FOOTPRINTS IN ENGLAND WERE FOUND IN HAPPISBURGH IN NORFOLK – AND THEY ARE BELIEVED TO BE AROUND 800,000 YEARS OLD, PROVING THAT PEOPLE LIVED IN ENGLAND EVEN THEN!

THE BAYEUX TAPESTRY, DEPICTING THE BATTLE OF HASTINGS IN 1066

1603–1714 The Stuarts
1714–1837 The Georgians
1837–1901 The Victorians
1901–1914 The Edwardian Era

LANDMARKS

England is full of famous <u>landmarks</u> which attract millions of visitors every year. They tell the story of the history of England, as well as shaping the landscape. Some of them, such as the Houses of Parliament in London or the Angel of the North in Gateshead, are made by humans.

Many of England's landmarks are natural, including the famous White Cliffs of Dover and the beautiful Lake District.

THE LAKE DISTRICT IS AN AREA OF OUTSTANDING NATURAL BEAUTY IN THE NORTH OF ENGLAND.

IT IS THOUGHT THAT THE CONSTRUCTION OF STONEHENGE BEGAN IN 3000 BC, BUT SOME OF THE STONES ARE SO HUGE AND SO HEAVY THAT SCIENTISTS, ARCHAEOLOGISTS AND ENGINEERS HAVE BEEN SCRATCHING THEIR HEADS FOR MANY, MANY YEARS TRYING TO WORK OUT HOW THEY GOT THERE!

STONEHENGE IS A CIRCLE OF ENORMOUS STANDING STONES IN WILTSHIRE.

TAKE A LOOK For lots of information about famous landmarks in England, take a look at www.english-heritage.org.uk or www.nationaltrust.org.uk

HADRIAN'S WALL IS ABOUT 118 KILOMETRES LONG AND ROUGHLY DIVIDES ENGLAND AND SCOTLAND. IT WAS BUILT HUNDREDS OF YEARS AGO BY THE ROMANS TO KEEP THE TRIBES IN THE NORTH FROM ATTACKING THE ROMAN SETTLEMENTS.

Some of the most famous landmarks in history are also the most mysterious and leave historians baffled and searching for answers. Stonehenge and the Uffington White Horse, which is carved into a hillside in Oxfordshire, are landmarks which are still surrounded by mystery.

THE FAMOUS GHERKIN BUILDING IN LONDON IS 180 METRES HIGH.

WEATHER & LANDSCAPE

England is famous for changeable weather. England's summers can be cooler than in some parts of Europe, but the winter can be warmer. One of the reasons for this is that England is part of an island which is influenced by a warm ocean current called the Gulf Stream.

England's landscape is very varied. Much of it is coastline, with famous coastal features such as the White Cliffs of Dover in Kent. There are hilly areas and stunning lakes in the Lake District, chalk hills in central and southern England, and areas of wide, flat land in East Anglia.

ENGLAND'S LOWEST POINT IS THE FENS IN EAST ANGLIA, WITH SOME AREAS BELOW THE LEVEL OF THE SEA.

ENGLAND HAS BECOME SLIGHTLY WETTER OVER THE LAST 30 YEARS — ANNUAL RAINFALL HAS INCREASED FROM 915 MILLIMETRES (MM) TO 926 MM.

TAKE A LOOK For information about some of England's landscapes to visit, look at www.nationaltrust.org.uk

Much of the countryside is used for **agriculture**, either arable (such as grains and vegetable crops) or animal farming. It is an important industry for the country as a whole.

According to the experts at Ordnance Survey (the guys that do the maps), the place in England that is farthest from the sea is Church Flatts Farm in a village called Cotton in the Elms in Derbyshire. It is nearly 113 km from the nearest coast.

England's highest point is Scafell Pike in the Lake District which stands at over 978 metres above sea level!

TOWNS & CITIES

Most people in England live in towns or cities. England's capital city, London, is the biggest city in the country, and is seen as one of the most famous and important cities in the world for business and culture.

OVER 8 MILLION PEOPLE LIVE IN LONDON.

Some of England's other largest cities are Birmingham, Leeds, Liverpool, and Sheffield. All four of these are in the north of England.

BIRMINGHAM LEEDS LIVERPOOL SHEFFIELD

Reading in Berkshire is England's biggest town, with a population of over 200,000.

Wells in Somerset is England's smallest city, with a population of over 10,000.

TAKE A LOOK — For information about some of the towns and cities of England, look at www.visitbritain.com

There are more than 50 cities and over 1,000 towns in England. The definition of a city is usually somewhere that has a cathedral, but sometimes the status of city is granted by the monarch. A town is generally a large, built-up settlement that is larger than a village but smaller in size than a city.

THE LIVER BIRDS ARE ONE OF THE MOST FAMOUS SIGHTS IN LIVERPOOL, ONE OF ENGLAND'S BIGGEST CITIES.

ELY CATHEDRAL

THERE IS A PLACE CALLED LEEDS WHICH IS A CITY, A PLACE CALLED LEEDS WHICH IS A VILLAGE IN KENT, AND A PLACE CALLED LEEDSTOWN, WHICH IS A VILLAGE IN CORNWALL! CHECK YOUR MAPS BEFORE YOU VISIT...

13

THE COUNTRYSIDE & WILDLIFE

England's countryside consists of areas of forest, marshlands, moorlands, mountains and lakes. Some of this land is used for agriculture, which is important to the economy and provides work and food for the population.

There are lots of different types of crops grown in England ranging from vegetables such as potatoes and sugar beet to grains such as wheat and barley. Animal farmers raise animals such as sheep, pigs and cows for food.

FARMING AND AGRICULTURE MAKES MORE THAN 8 BILLION POUNDS FOR THE UK ECONOMY.

COWS ON FARMS ARE KNOWN AS 'CATTLE'.

TAKE A LOOK For information about the countryside visit www.hedgelink.org.uk and www.wildengland.com

THERE ARE AROUND 1,500 DIFFERENT SPECIES OF INSECT LIVING IN HEDGEROWS ACROSS THE COUNTRY.

RAPESEED IS A COMMON CROP FOR FARMERS TO GROW. AS WELL AS BEING USED IN FOOD AND COOKING OILS IT CAN BE USED AS FUEL TO RUN CARS AND OTHER VEHICLES.

The countryside is important for wildlife, and there are thousands of different species of plants, flowers, birds and small animals that depend on hedgerows, forests, rivers and open spaces for survival.

THE SMALLEST BIRD IN ENGLAND IS THE GOLDCREST, WHICH IS JUST NINE CENTIMETRES (CM) LONG!

SMALL ANIMALS, SUCH AS MICE, LIVE IN THE FIELDS AND HEDGEROWS OF ENGLAND'S COUNTRYSIDE.

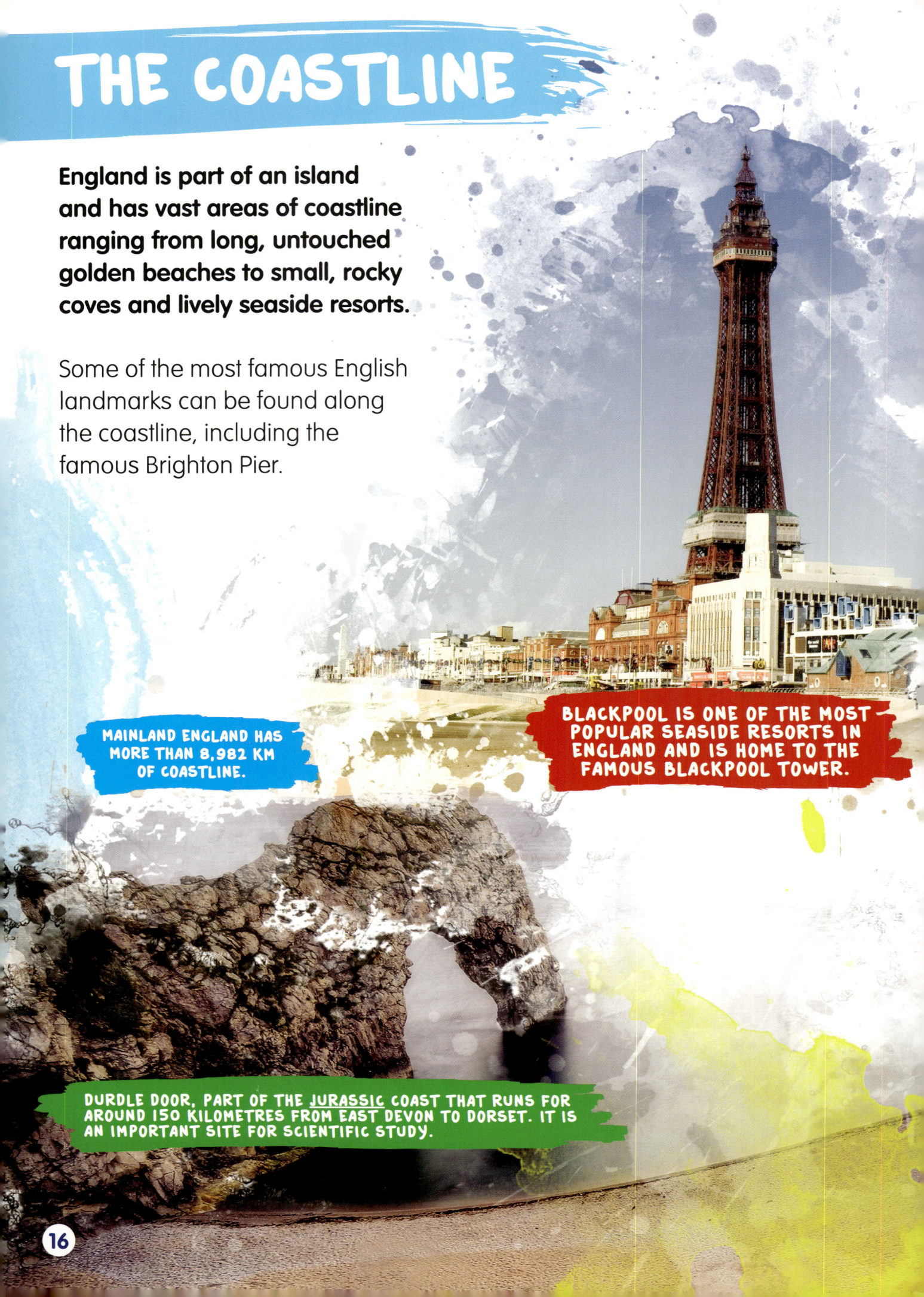

THE COASTLINE

England is part of an island and has vast areas of coastline ranging from long, untouched golden beaches to small, rocky coves and lively seaside resorts.

Some of the most famous English landmarks can be found along the coastline, including the famous Brighton Pier.

MAINLAND ENGLAND HAS MORE THAN 8,982 KM OF COASTLINE.

BLACKPOOL IS ONE OF THE MOST POPULAR SEASIDE RESORTS IN ENGLAND AND IS HOME TO THE FAMOUS BLACKPOOL TOWER.

DURDLE DOOR, PART OF THE JURASSIC COAST THAT RUNS FOR AROUND 150 KILOMETRES FROM EAST DEVON TO DORSET. IT IS AN IMPORTANT SITE FOR SCIENTIFIC STUDY.

TAKE A LOOK For information about coastal wildlife visit www.ypte.org.uk/factsheets/seashore/life-in-a-rock-pool and for information about the Jurassic Coast visit www.jurassiccoast.org

The English coastline attracts many **tourists** from all over the world. Tourism is important for the economy because it creates jobs for lots of people living and working in towns and villages by the sea. It is also important as it can help people to learn about the history and geography of England.

The coastline is shaped by the force of the wind, rain and waves which constantly hit and eventually break up the rocks. This means that the coastline is changing every single day.

MARTELLO TOWERS LIKE THIS ONE WERE BUILT ALONG THE ENGLISH COASTLINE IN THE 1800s TO PROTECT ENGLAND FROM INVASION BY FRANCE.

IN 2010, A MONSTER CRAB WAS CAUGHT BY FISHERMEN OFF THE COAST OF FALMOUTH IN CORNWALL. IT WAS AROUND 60 CM LONG FROM CLAW TO CLAW AND WEIGHED A WHOPPING 3.5 KILOGRAMS AND WAS BELIEVED TO HAVE BEEN ABOUT 20 YEARS OLD.

PEOPLE

Over half of England's population are Christian. Many other people follow different religions including Judaism, Islam and Hinduism. Many also follow no religion at all.

The population of England is made up of people from many different cultures who live side by side in its towns, cities and villages.

Most people live long, healthy lives and are able to work, which makes England a popular destination for **immigrants**.

CITY

TOWN

VILLAGE

TAKE A LOOK

For more fun facts and information about England, visit
www.sciencekids.co.nz/sciencefacts/countries/england.html

THERE ARE MORE PEOPLE OVER 60 IN ENGLAND THAN UNDER THE AGE OF 16.

THE LIFE EXPECTANCY OF SOMEONE BORN IN ENGLAND IS AROUND 80 YEARS.

Children in England start school around the age of five. Some go to state schools, which are funded by the government. Others go to public schools, which are paid for by their families.

PRINCE HARRY AND PRINCE WILLIAM WENT TO A PRIVATE SCHOOL CALLED ETON, AS DID THE ACTOR EDDIE REDMAYNE, OLYMPIC GOLD MEDALIST SIR MATTHEW PINSENT, ADVENTURER BEAR GRYLLS AND MANY OTHER FAMOUS PEOPLE.

19

CULTURE, LEISURE & TOURISM

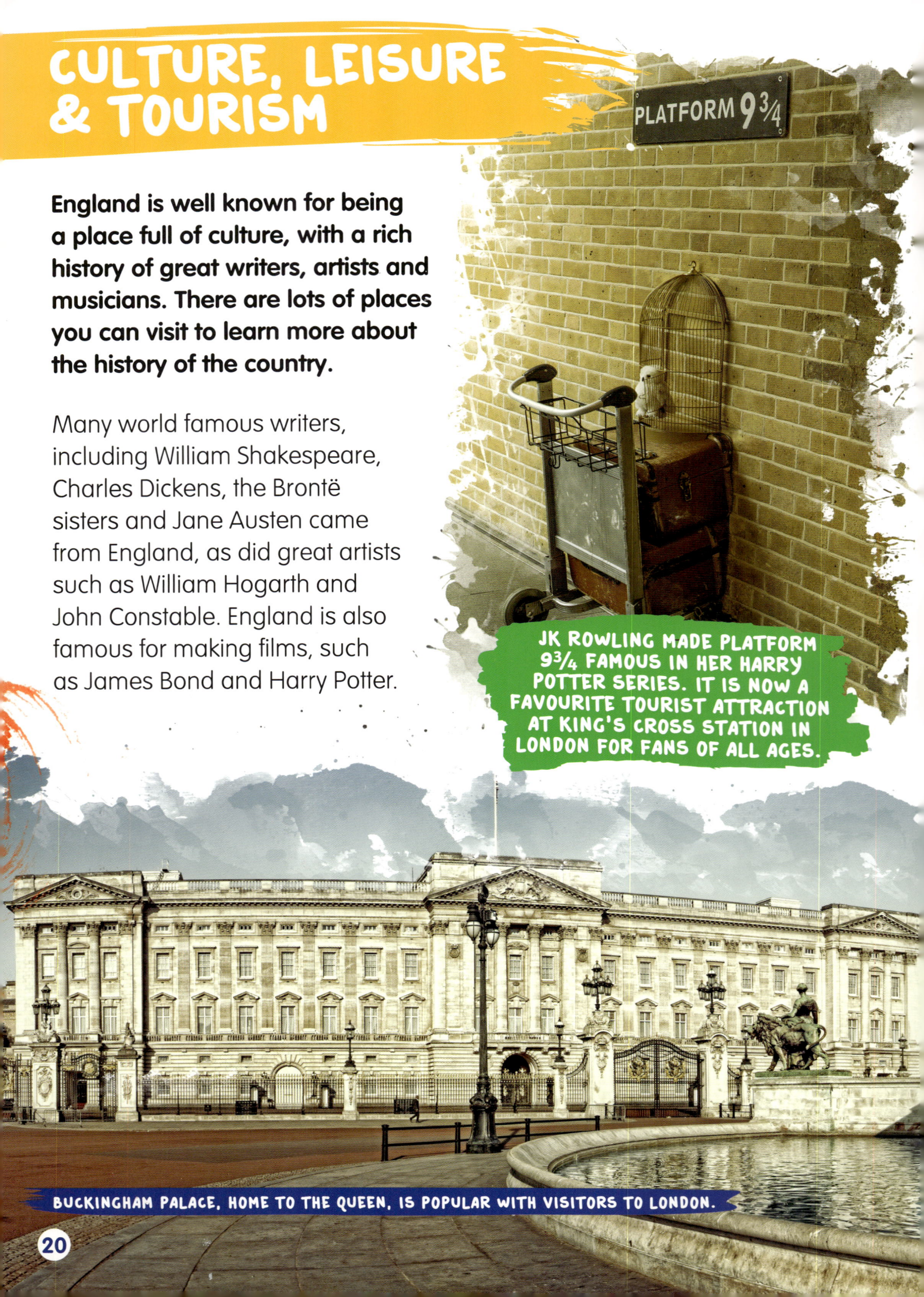

England is well known for being a place full of culture, with a rich history of great writers, artists and musicians. There are lots of places you can visit to learn more about the history of the country.

Many world famous writers, including William Shakespeare, Charles Dickens, the Brontë sisters and Jane Austen came from England, as did great artists such as William Hogarth and John Constable. England is also famous for making films, such as James Bond and Harry Potter.

JK ROWLING MADE PLATFORM 9¾ FAMOUS IN HER HARRY POTTER SERIES. IT IS NOW A FAVOURITE TOURIST ATTRACTION AT KING'S CROSS STATION IN LONDON FOR FANS OF ALL AGES.

BUCKINGHAM PALACE, HOME TO THE QUEEN, IS POPULAR WITH VISITORS TO LONDON.

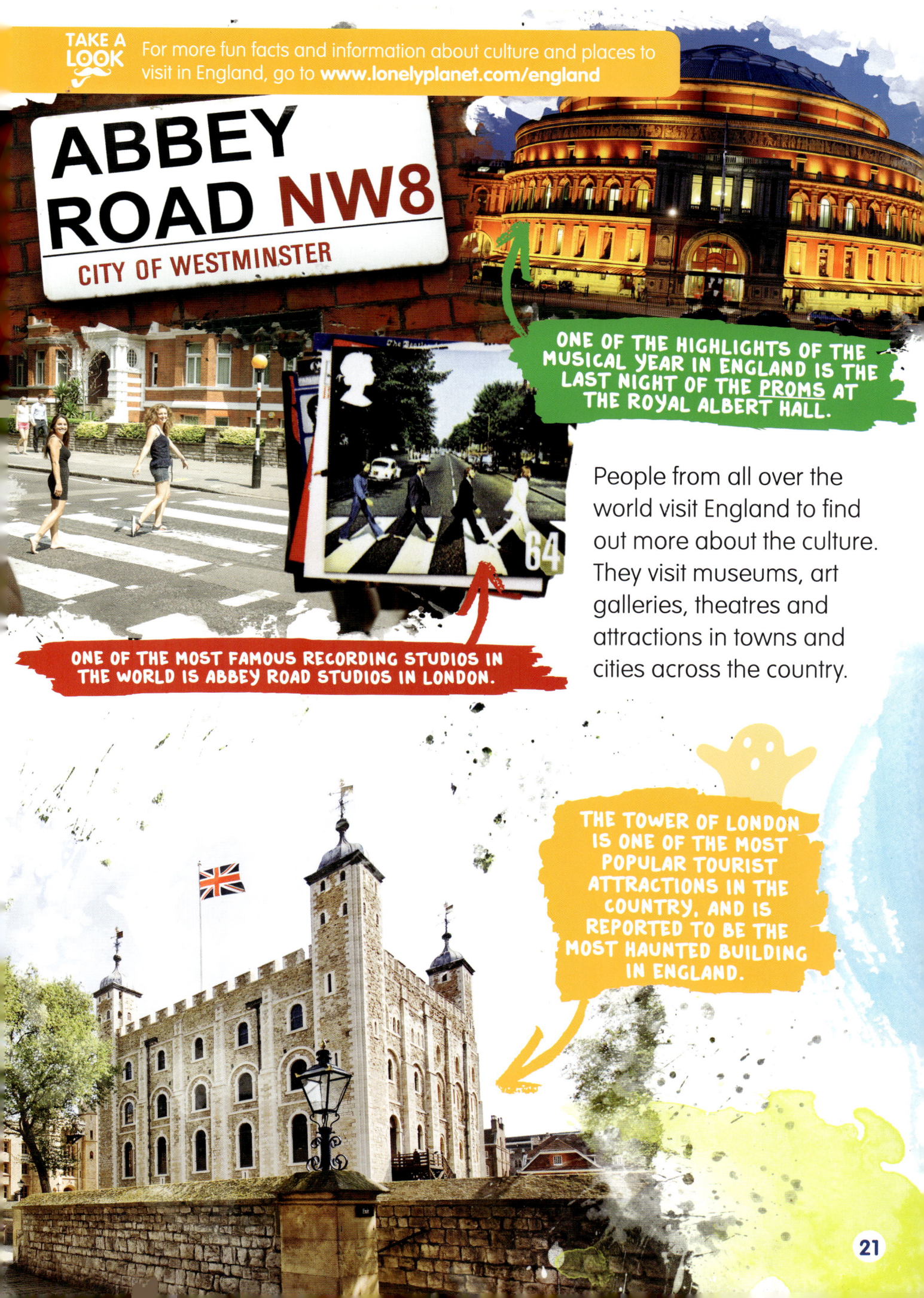

TAKE A LOOK For more fun facts and information about culture and places to visit in England, go to www.lonelyplanet.com/england

ABBEY ROAD NW8
CITY OF WESTMINSTER

ONE OF THE HIGHLIGHTS OF THE MUSICAL YEAR IN ENGLAND IS THE LAST NIGHT OF THE PROMS AT THE ROYAL ALBERT HALL.

People from all over the world visit England to find out more about the culture. They visit museums, art galleries, theatres and attractions in towns and cities across the country.

ONE OF THE MOST FAMOUS RECORDING STUDIOS IN THE WORLD IS ABBEY ROAD STUDIOS IN LONDON.

THE TOWER OF LONDON IS ONE OF THE MOST POPULAR TOURIST ATTRACTIONS IN THE COUNTRY, AND IS REPORTED TO BE THE MOST HAUNTED BUILDING IN ENGLAND.

21

SPORT

WEMBLEY STADIUM IS HOME TO ENGLAND'S FOOTBALL TEAM, BUT IS ALSO USED FOR OTHER SPORTS AND FOR CONCERTS.

From Wimbledon to Wembley, England has a rich sporting history and is home to some of the most famous stadiums and sporting arenas in the world.

In 2012, England hosted the Olympic Games and the Olympic Park was built in east London to host the games. Millions of people visited the country to watch athletes from around the world compete in 26 different sports.

THE TOUR DE FRANCE, A FAMOUS CYCLE RACE, CAME TO ENGLAND IN 2014.

THE WIMBLEDON TENNIS CHAMPIONSHIP IS ONE OF THE MOST FAMOUS TENNIS TOURNAMENTS IN THE WORLD.

TAKE A LOOK

For more fun facts and information about sport in England, visit www.sportengland.org

MANY BELIEVE THAT RUGBY WAS INVENTED IN 1823 WHEN A SCHOOLBOY CALLED WILLIAM WEBB ELLIS PICKED UP A FOOTBALL AND RAN WITH IT IN HIS ARMS.

England is famous for many sports and professional sportspeople. Many English people take part in sport for **leisure**, and are members of sports clubs and teams.

THERE IS EVIDENCE OF CRICKET BEING PLAYED IN ENGLAND AS FAR BACK AS 1550!

TRADITIONS

England and English people are sometimes seen as quirky and different by people from other countries because of some of their unusual traditions.

From cheese rolling competitions, bog snorkelling and eel throwing to dancing at the Last Night of the Proms, there are many different traditional activities that have been enjoyed for centuries.

REMEMBER, REMEMBER THE 5TH OF NOVEMBER — EVERY YEAR PEOPLE ACROSS THE COUNTRY CELEBRATE THE ANNIVERSARY OF GUY FAWKES, WHO TRIED TO BLOW UP THE HOUSES OF PARLIAMENT IN 1605.

TAKE A LOOK For more fun facts, strange customs and traditions visit www.cntraveller.com/recommended/uk/strange-customs-english-traditions-weird-events

EVERY YEAR ON THE 1ST OF MAY PEOPLE ACROSS ENGLAND DANCE AROUND MAYPOLES TO CELEBRATE THE START OF SPRING.

Some traditions, such as the daily 'Changing the Guard' at Buckingham Palace, are especially popular with tourists.

THE QUEEN'S GUARDS AT BUCKINGHAM PALACE WEAR TRADITIONAL TUNICS AND BEARSKIN HATS.

QUICK QUIZ

Have you been paying attention? Let's find out!
Take the quick quiz to see how much you have found out in this book.

1. WHAT IS THE POPULATION OF ENGLAND?
2. HOW MANY KILOMETRES OF COASTLINE DOES ENGLAND HAVE?
3. WHERE IS THE LOWEST POINT IN ENGLAND?
4. WHERE IS THE ANGEL OF THE NORTH?
5. HOW FAR FROM THE SEA IS CHURCH FLATTS FARM?
6. WHERE IS SCAFELL PIKE?
7. WHERE WOULD YOU FIND THE LIVER BIRDS?
8. WHAT IS THE SMALLEST BIRD IN ENGLAND?
9. APART FROM MAKING COOKING OIL, WHAT ELSE IS RAPESEED USED FOR?
10. HOW HEAVY WAS THE MONSTER CRAB?

11. **WHAT IS THE LIFE EXPECTANCY OF SOMEONE BORN IN ENGLAND?**

12. **WHERE IS PLATFORM 9¾?**

13. **WHAT SCHOOL DID PRINCE HARRY GO TO?**

14. **WHAT YEAR DID ENGLAND HOST THE OLYMPIC GAMES?**

15. **WHERE IS THE GHERKIN?**

16. **ON WHAT DAY OF THE YEAR DO PEOPLE DANCE AROUND A MAYPOLE?**

17. **HOW MANY PEOPLE LIVE IN LONDON?**

18. **HOW MANY CITIES ARE THERE IN ENGLAND?**

19. **WHY WAS HADRIAN'S WALL BUILT?**

20. **WHAT IS THOUGHT TO BE THE MOST HAUNTED BUILDING IN ENGLAND?**

ANSWERS:

1) 55,750,000
2) 8,982 KM
3) THE FENS, EAST ANGLIA
4) GATESHEAD
5) 113 KM
6) THE LAKE DISTRICT
7) LIVERPOOL
8) GOLDCREST
9) TO MAKE FUEL
10) 3.5 KILOGRAMS
11) AROUND 80 YEARS
12) KING'S CROSS STATION, LONDON
13) ETON
14) 2012
15) LONDON
16) THE 1ST OF MAY
17) OVER 8 MILLION
18) MORE THAN 50
19) TO STOP TRIBES IN THE NORTH FROM ATTACKING ROMAN SETTLEMENTS
20) THE TOWER OF LONDON

USEFUL LINKS

Useful websites to help you find out more about England

www.lonelyplanet.com/england

www.tourist-information-uk.com

www.visitbritain.com

www.infoplease.com/country/united-kingdom.html

kids.nationalgeographic.com/explore/countries/united-kingdom/

www.bbc.co.uk/history/british/launch_tl_british.shtml

www.nationaltrust.org.uk

www.english-heritage.org.uk

www.wildlifetrusts.org

www.hedgelink.org.uk

www.wildengland.com

PLACES TO VISIT

Interesting places to visit in England

THE BRITISH MUSEUM
www.britishmuseum.org

THE NATURAL HISTORY MUSEUM
www.nhm.ac.uk

SUTTON HOO
www.nationaltrust.org.uk/sutton-hoo

STONEHENGE
www.english-heritage.org.uk/stonehenge

HADRIAN'S WALL
www.english-heritage.org.uk/visit/places/hadrians-wall

BATH
www.visitbath.co.uk

THE WHITE CLIFFS OF DOVER
www.nationaltrust.org.uk/white-cliffs-dover

THE LAKE DISTRICT
www.lakedistrict.gov.uk

THE MUSEUM OF SCIENCE AND INDUSTRY
www.scienceandindustrymuseum.org.uk

THE OXFORD UNIVERSITY MUSEUM OF NATURAL HISTORY
www.oum.ox.ac.uk

THE MUSEUM OF ENGLISH RURAL LIFE
www.reading.ac.uk/merl

THE SCIENCE MUSEUM
www.sciencemuseum.org.uk

WEMBLEY STADIUM
www.wembleystadium.com

THE JURASSIC COAST
www.jurassiccoast.org

GLOSSARY

AD	after the birth of Jesus, which is used as the starting point for many calendars around the world
AGRICULTURE	farming of either crops or animals
BAYEAUX TAPESTRY	a very large piece of cloth with lots of detailed scenes sewn into it that show the events leading up to and including the battle of 1066
BC	meaning 'before Christ', is used to mark dates that occurred before the starting year of most calendars
BILLION	a thousand million
CULTURE	a way of life and traditions of a group of people
CURRENCY	the money a country uses
ECONOMY	the way trade and money is controlled by a country
HEAD OF STATE	the public leader of a country
IMMIGRANTS	people from other countries who go to live and work in another country
JURASSIC	a period of time that lasted from 199.6 million to 145.5 million years ago
LANDMARKS	places or buildings that are easily recognised
LANDSCAPES	physical features such as mountains, rivers, hills or coastlines
LEISURE	what people do in their spare time
LIFE EXPECTANCY	how long a person is expected to live
MONARCH	a king or queen
PROMS	an annual event held at the Albert Hall in London featuring a series of musical concerts
TOURISTS	people who visit a place for pleasure

INDEX

AGRICULTURE	11, 14
ANGLO SAXONS	6
ANIMALS	11, 14-15
ARTISTS	20
CITIES	4-5, 12-13, 18, 21
COASTLINE	5, 10, 16-17, 29
COUNTRYSIDE	5, 11, 14-15
CROPS	11, 14-15
CULTURE	5, 12, 18, 20-21
HEDGEROWS	15, 28
HISTORY	5-9, 20, 22, 28-29
LANDMARKS	8-9, 16
LANDSCAPES	5, 8, 10-11
PEOPLE	6-7, 12, 17-19, 21-25
POPULATION	4, 12, 14, 18
ROMANS	6, 9
SCHOOL	19, 23
SPORT	5, 22-23
TOURISM	17, 20-21, 25
TOWNS	5, 12-13, 17-18, 21
TRADITIONS	5, 24-25
VIKINGS	6
VILLAGES	5, 11, 13, 17-18
WILDLIFE	14-15, 17, 28
WRITERS	20

Photo credits: Abbreviations: l-left, r-right, b-bottom, t-top, c-centre, m-middle, bg-background. Images are courtesy of Shutterstock.com. With thanks to Getty Images, Thinkstock Photo and iStockphoto. Front Cover: tl – PHB.cz (Richard Semik), tr – RonFromYork, ml – Stephen Gibson, mr – Justin Black, bl – Fulcanelli, br – Jaroslaw Grudzinski. 3t – Diego Barbieri, 3b – stocksolutions, 4back – okili77, 4 front – tanatat, 5t: l – Stewart Smith Photography; cl – QQ7; c – Helen Hotson; cr – ian woolcock, r – Kanuman, m – Andy Lidstone, b – PHOTOCREO Michal Bednarek, 6t – Featureflash, 6b – Justin Black, 7tl – milias1987, 7tr – Ivan Ponomarev, b – jorisvo, 8t – Undivided, 8/9b – Fulcanelli, 9tl – PHB.cz (Richard Semik), 9tr – Hal_P, 9m – Dave Price, 10t – Platslee, 10b – Tamara Kulikova, 11 – Stewart Smith Photography, 12l – Tupungato, 12cl – Shahid Khan, 12cr – JuliusKielaitis, 12 – Shahid Khan, 13bg – Patricia Hofmeester, 13mr – chrisdorney, 14 – David Hughes, 15t – Petr Kopka, 15b – Charles Masters, 16tr – Stephen Gibson, 16b – Lukasz Pajor, 17t – DavidYoung, 17b – LovArt, 18t – Rawpixel.com, 18b: l – MJSquared Photography, c – 1000 Words, r – JeniFoto, 19t – Goodluz, 19 c – caranto, 19b – Monkey Business Images, 20t – patronestaff, 20b – r.nagy, 21tl – Tutti Frutti, 21tr – Dan Breckwoldt, ml – Brian S, mc – Neftali, 21b – Justin Black, 22t – majeczka, 22ml – Leonard Zhukovsky, 22bl – catwalker, 22br – Lucy Clark, 23t – Paolo Bona, 23bl – Philip Bird LRPS CPAGB, 23br – Mark Lorch, 24t – Lance Bellers, 24b – Bikeworldtravel, 25t – Oscar Johns, 25b – padchas.

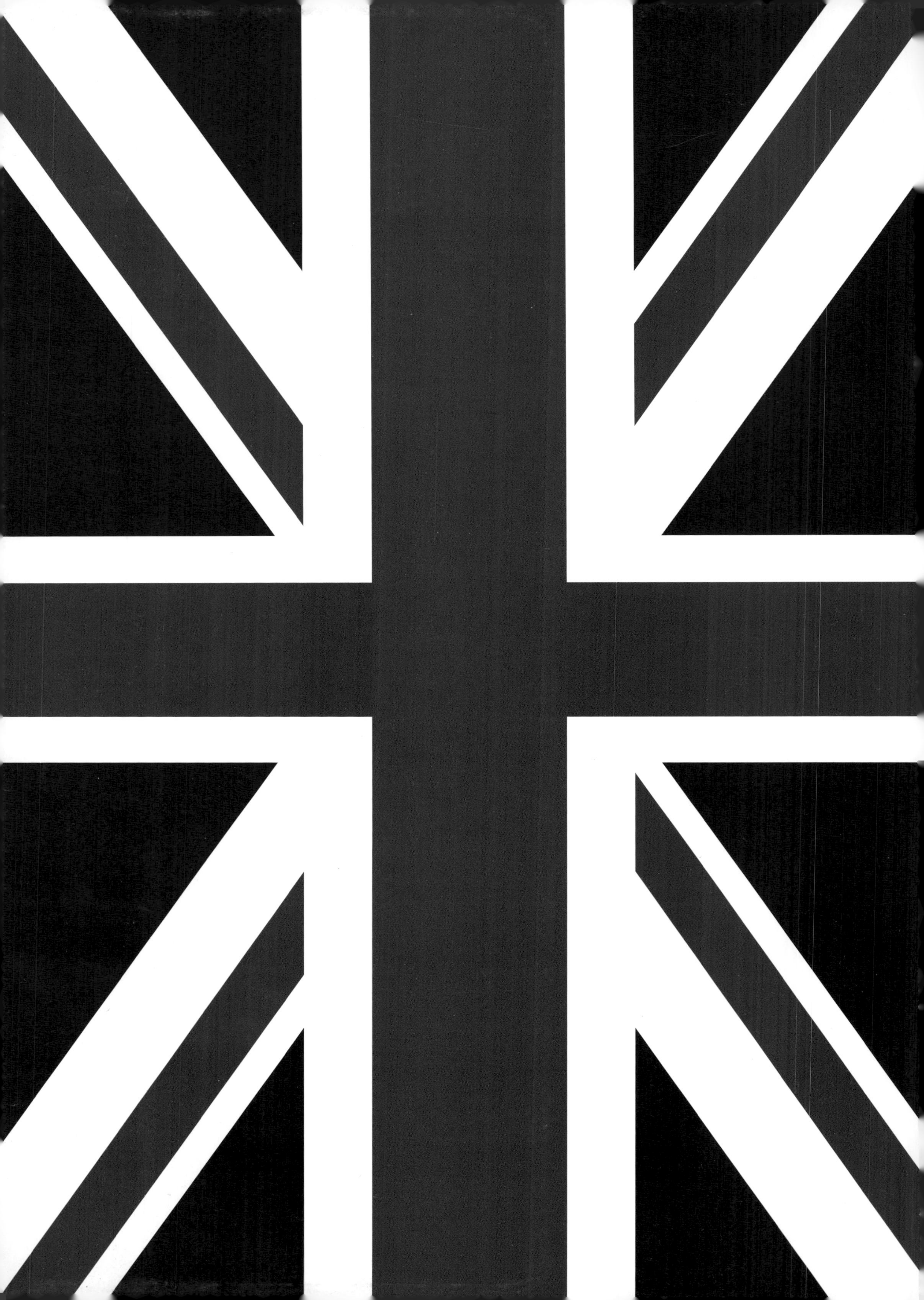